Chicago

Irving Weisdorf & Co. Ltd.

Chicago's stunning skyline.

INTRODUCTION

For more than a century, Chicago has been known as the "Windy City" although the phrase wasn't originally coined to describe the weather. Rather, it was New York Sun editor Charles Dana's reference to the city's long-winded politicians.

When looking at downtown Chicago today, it's hard to imagine that at one time the Illinois Indians lived here, on the shores of Lake Michigan. The area was known to them as "Chicaugou". The name may mean powerful, strong or great, but there's also a chance it stands for skunk or big smell, as this portage point smelled strongly of the wild onions that dotted the area. It was to this mudflat, at the mouth of a three-pronged river, that famed French explorers Jolliet and Marquette first visited and discovered what is now Chicago. They were eventually followed by the French who established a settlement in the 1770s.

An official city since 1837, Chicago is an exciting, dynamic place that offers a variety of urban amenities, culture, entertainment and sport. It is a cosmopolitan city, made up of many distinctive neighborhoods and is often referred to as the heart of the Midwest. Its miles of glass, concrete and steel are balanced by a multitude of parks, forest preserve, rivers and, of course, the accessible waterfront of Great Lake Michigan.

Chicago is the third largest metropolitan area in the U.S. and has the third largest population of more than seven million people. It's a friendly place with something special for everyone. There's much to be a part of in Chicago and this spirited city is always ready to impress its visitors. A Chicago experience is a unique experience. It's big, busy and beautiful.

Chicago is a city of firsts, with the first ferris wheel, stainless steel building, bifocal contact lens, caramel-chocolate turtles, Cracker Jacks and totally fire-proof hotel, the Palmer House Hilton. Chicago's own Jane Addams, founder of the Hull House which opened in 1889 to provide aid to Chicago immigrants, was the first American woman to win the Nobel Prize for Peace in 1931. The first regulation baseballs and bats were manufactured by Chicago entrepreneur and former pitcher Albert G. Spalding. Chicago gave us "Dear Abby," the Sears Catalogue and "New York Cut" steaks. Finally, and not surprisingly, Chicago is the site of the first skyscraper.

The Home Insurance Building, erected by architect Major William Le Baron Jenney at the northeast corner of LaSalle and Adams streets in 1885, was the world's first skyscraper. It is no longer there, and even if it were it would not compare to the skyscrapers of today. But this building, an amazing architectural feat for its time, had nine stories and one basement.

The Wrigley Building and The Tribune Tower on the north bank of the Chicago River.

After Jenney's accomplishment, the sky was truly the limit for building. His first skyscraper revolutionized urban life because with higher buildings, many people could live and work in more concentrated areas — and that's what people do quite successfully in Chicago today.

Looking north at sunrise along the lakeshore to the Drake Hotel where the Magnificent Mile ends and the Gold Coast begins.

Two classic downtown office buildings on Michigan Avenue are the well-known **Wrigley Building** and the **Tribune Tower**. Many consider them the most famous architectural landmarks in Chicago today.

HISTORY

On Oct. 8, 1871, **The Great Chicago Fire** destroyed the bulk of the city's center. It started in the lumber district on the city's west side, but many still blame old Lady Leary's cow for kicking over the kerosene lamp and igniting the blaze. Whether or not the fire really started in the barn on DeKoven St., it was definitely one of the first buildings to succumb to the flames. The fire jumped the river, spreading to the south side. A light rain 25 hours later kept the flames from spreading, but after two days it had flattened close to four square miles. The fire killed at least 300 people and left 100,000 homeless. More than 18,000 buildings were destroyed and property damage was estimated at $200-million.

It was then that The Chicago Tribune issued the challenge, "Let the watchword henceforth be, Chicago shall rise again." And rise again Chicago did. In fact, the city soared as internationally acclaimed architects flocked to the metropolis to participate in the reconstruction.

These late 19th-century architects, along with many engineers, faced the challenges and overcame the obstacles of rebuilding a city that had originally been swampland. The structural innovations included steel beams, concrete rafts and iron cages. Among the architects who put their stamp on the rebuilt city were Louis Sullivan, William Jenney, John M. Van Osdel and later Frank Lloyd Wright and Mies van der Rohe.

Chicago's reputation as a commercial center grew quickly in the early 1900s. State Street helped earn that reputation.
State Street today runs across town and straight through the heart of downtown Chicago or "The Loop," and is one of the world's most famous streets. It is part of the very important business and tourist district of downtown Chicago and is the address to many popular and exciting places including the Chicago Theatre, the American Police Center and Museum, the Embassy Suites Hotel and one of the world's largest public libraries, the Harold Washington Library Center. State Street may be most known and loved for its world-class shopping which includes the famous Carson Pirie Scott and Company and Marshall Field and Company. Chicago's street numbers originate at the intersection of State and Madison streets. State Street divides east and west addresses with 100 numbers to each city block — a long way from the State Street of the early 1900s.

(right) The Great Chicago Fire decimated the city in 1871. Although church walls were left the standing, the City Hall was virtually reduced to rubble (below).

(left) The wholesale produce market was a hive of activity, while Humboldt Park (above) provided a tranquil haven for city dwellers.

Where there's a river, there are bridges – and Chicago is no exception. Road traffic must give the right-of-way to boats when the barriers come down on Michigan Avenue, Kinzie Street, Clark Street, or Wabash Avenue bridges. There are, in fact, 52 movable bridges in Chicago, more than any other city in the world.

For a city that had originally been swampland, today Chicago has the beautiful characteristics of water. Lake Michigan and the **Chicago River** make for a great many delightful sights and activities.

Chicago's waters have interesting stories and histories, especially the Chicago River, which flowed in the opposite direction to which it does today. The sewage system of early Chicago was primitive, running sewage directly into Lake Michigan or the Chicago River which ran directly into the lake. The system eventually led to a state of emergency due to the polluted waters, resulting in many deaths and diseases. In 1987, Rudolph Hering, chief engineer of the drainage and water supply commission, decided that a bold engineering feat to reverse the Chicago River was the answer to their emergency, and it was. A drainage and shipping channel was built from the south branch of the Chicago River which has flowed backward ever since.

In what has become a time-honored tradition, a pipefitters union has been dyeing the Chicago River green on St. Patrick's Day every year. The harmless dye produces a very spectacular sight, attracting more visitors to the river than any other time of year.

Carp and goldfish make up a large portion of the Chicago River's population, although over 50 species of fish, including trout and salmon, have been identified in the varied reaches of the river. There have even been reported sightings of beaver, muskrat, and mink on the river.

The **Michigan Avenue Bridge,** which spans the Chicago River, tells the historical story of the city through the sculptures on the four pylons of the bridge. The sculptures represent major Chicago events: its discovery by Marquette and Jolliet, its settlement by du Sable, the fort Dearborn Massacre of 1812, and the rebuilding of the city after the Great Chicago Fire in 1871. These sculptures, by James Earle Fraser and Henry Hering, were added to the four bridgehouses eight years after the bridge was completed.

The sunrise reflects off the Chicago River.

The river affords spectacular city views and celebrated riverside architecture.

The Michigan Avenue Bridge leads to many notable skyscrapers. The **Wrigley Building,** on the west side of Michigan Avenue, is one of the most distinguished buildings in Chicago. Not only is it beautiful and distinctly different, it is also the corporate home of the Wrigley chewing-gum empire.

The Wrigley Building was built by the same architectural firm that designed the Merchandise Mart and Union Station, but has a look all its own. Its fine Spanish Renaissance structure is based upon the Giralda Tower of Seville. The building actually consists of two structures. The south tower was completed in 1921 and William Wrigley considered it to be such a success that he asked for a second building, with twice the floor space as the first, to be built. The second structure was completed in 1924. With its white terra cotta exterior and enormous clock on the **clock tower,** the Wrigley Building is impossible to overlook.

The Wrigley Building's clock tower is a cherished landmark.

This powerful sculptural relief panel, by James Earle Fraser, celebrates Chicago's early history and graces the Michigan Avenue Bridge at the Chicago River.

As magnificent as the Wrigley Building is, it isn't the only structure to turn heads in Chicago. Many visitors comment on and remember what has been nicknamed the two "corncobs". This twin-like structure, at 300 North State, is a part of architect Bertrand Goldberg's **Marina City** — the residential and water-recreation complex. This complex, on the north bank of the Chicago River, was a popular address for the area's young professionals when it was first built in the 1960s. Today it is known not only as Chicago's tallest concrete structure, at 62 storeys, but as a multi-use complex that includes: wedge-shaped apartments, offices, restaurants, 18 storeys of parking, a theater, an ice rink and a marina.

The "corncobs" make a nice backdrop for the very famous statue of **George Washington** that stands across the river at Herald Square. The statue shows Washington clasping the hands of his American Revolution supporters, Robert Morris and Hyam Salomon.

Yet another striking building in the area, built in dramatic Gothic Revival style in 1925, is the **Chicago Tribune Tower.** It was once the winning design of an international competition. Authentic pieces of famous buildings such as Westminster Abbey, the Great Pyramids and the Taj Mahal are embedded in its walls.

George Washington stands, bronzed forever, clasping the hands of Robert Morris and Hyam Salomon — his two financial supporters in the American Revolution. This memorial, now designated a Chicago Landmark, was presented to the city in 1941 by a group of civic leaders who commissioned Lorado Taft to design a tribute to these patriots. Taft did not live to see his design erected in Herald Square — he died leaving the sculpture to be completed by his associate Leonard Crunelle.

Behind the memorial are the twin towers, or "corncobs," of Marina City. They are residential skyscrapers, prestigiously situated beside the river. These sixty stories are some of Chicago's most uniquely designed, featuring pie-shaped rooms and semi-circular balconies. The lower floors of the buildings contain parking lots and a shopping complex.

The Tribune Tower.

"Monument with Standing Beast," by French artist Jean Dubuffet, stands near the entrance to the James R. Thompson Center.

Interior of James R. Thompson Center.

ARCHITECTURE

There is much to appreciate when it comes to Chicago's architecture. Just a sweeping view of the city reveals architecture that is diverse, ranging from the elegantly ornate to the stunningly simple. The buildings reflect a citizenry interested in preserving the traditional while showcasing the modern.

The best example of modern architecture in Chicago would have to be the **James R. Thompson Center** (formerly known as the State of Illinois Center). It was dedicated in 1985, by Governor James Thompson, as "The first building of the 21st century." Many love the much discussed building and many don't. But no one can argue the fact that it's different. Inside one can look up and see the sky, or take a ride up in one of the glass elevators to look down on Chicago's most invigorating interior space. A total architectural opposite to the center is the **Merchandise Mart,** built in 1930. This more traditional structure serves as one of the largest merchandising areas in the world.

Imposing on two full city blocks, the Merchandise Mart, a wholesale merchandising facility, has 7.5 miles of corridor.

SEARS TOWER

There's no better way to get an overall look at Chicago than from the 103rd floor of the **Sears Tower,** the world's tallest building. From the Skydeck Observatory, which is 1,353 feet above the streets of Chicago, visitors get a 360 degree view and can see for 60 miles on a clear day. Of course anyone wanting a view from the Skydeck must first ride the world's fastest elevator to get there.

The Sears Tower reaches 1,454 feet into the heavens and has 110 storeys. It also takes up 129,000 square feet on a city block. It's no wonder it took three years to build with 76,000 tons of steel and 16,000 bronze-tinted windows. The 56-foot-tall glass atrium at the main entrance to the Sears Tower is the result of a multimillion-dollar refurbishing in 1985. Also added at that time was a shopping mall and seven restaurants.

"The Loop," the heart of downtown and Chicago's historic business district, is a square mile surrounded by the routes of the elevated trains. The trains have been running this loop for almost a century.

(opposite page) William Pedersen designed 333 Wacker Drive to reflect the curve of the Chicago River, which it does in more ways than one. This curved building, completed in the mid-1980s, glistens as its mirrored exterior reflects the water, sky and surrounding buildings of Chicago. In contrast to many of the buildings in the city, this one does not need height to attract attention. The building is refreshingly distinctive and has earned considerable acclaim with its mosaic of mirrors that reflect the changing beauty of its surroundings.

Designed by Louis H. Sullivan and built at the "World's Busiest Corner," at Madison and State streets, is the Carson Pirie Scott & Co. store. It was the architect's last major commission and is decorated by elaborate cast iron work. In architectural circles, it is one of America's most highly regarded commercial structures.

John Hancock Center

If you're not convinced a view from the world's tallest building is the thing for you, maybe a trip up the world's fifth tallest building is better. The **John Hancock Center** is 1,127 feet high, not including the TV antennas. Its observatory offers a 60-mile view on a clear day from the 94th of 100 floors — 1,030 feet from street level.

The gracefully tapered John Hancock Center, with a distinctive X-frame structure, has crisscross braces which provide not only support in high winds, but a decorative element as well.

Close by the John Hancock Center is the **Water Tower,** which was one of the few buildings to survive the fire of 1871. The tower houses a 37-foot pipe that was once used to equalize the water pressure for the pumping station, which is across the street. Today both the Water Tower and Pumping Station are used by the Chicago Office of Tourism and the Visitors Center.

Chicago in new fallen snow, offers pictures of serenity.

Wintertime visitors to Chicago should arrive prepared for the cold as Chicago is capable of some raw weather and the occasional news-making blizzard. The city has also been known to have mild winters as well, so don't let the rumors keep you away. No amount of snow can cover Chicago's rich culture and grand sights.

The city's record low temperature was set on January 20, 1985 when the thermometer read 27 degrees Celsius below zero. The coldest winter was the winter of 1976/77 when the temperature remained below freezing for 43 consecutive days.

Two years later, during the winter of 1978/79, record snow falls hit Chicago. Over a three month period a heaping 89.7 inches of snow fell. The most snow ever accumulated during a single snowstorm in Chicago was in January 1967. In a little more than 24 hours, Chicago received 23 inches of snow which virtually stopped all action in the city for several days.

One advantage to visiting the city in the winter is the chance to see the lavish Christmas decorations in the stores of the Magnificent Mile and the State Street Mall. There's nothing like Christmas shopping in a big city — especially when that city is as big, beautiful and busy as Chicago is.

During any season, Chicago promises enough activities and attractions to keep any visitor happy and warm.

BEACHES

What would Chicago be like without Lake Michigan? Unimaginable!

The joy of living in and visiting Chicago owes a lot to the city's waterside location. It enjoys a highly accessible shoreline, where people gather and meet for rest and recreation. The Chicago Park District operates more than 30 beaches, along 20 miles of lakefront, most of which are sand or rock. The real estate on Lake Shore Drive is much desired and sells at a high price.

The swimming season in Chicago is from mid-June until early September. Most of the beaches have changing facilities and are protected by lifeguards during daylight hours in the swimming season. It is too cold to swim any other time of the year.

Lake Shore Drive, in Chicago, is one of the loveliest urban drives in the country. This comes thanks to a decision by city officials to ensure that the majority of the city's lakeside be devoted to parks and pleasure boats rather than to docks, warehouses and commercial activities. The city also improved this area with the replacement of the infamous Lake Shore Drive S-Curve. A gently curving roadway was the result of a four-year reconstruction project that cost $98-million. Begun in 1982, the new stretch of road was opened to northbound traffic in October, 1985 and to southbound traffic in November, 1986.

Of the approximate 12 million pleasure visitors to Chicago each year, it is almost guaranteed that all enjoy some aspect of the city's great Lake Michigan. The St. Lawrence Seaway connects Lake Michigan to the Atlantic making the city an international seaport. The lake is so large that to all intents and purposes it is a sea. There are piers for fishing, over 30 beaches, tables for chess and miles of sidewalk for strolling. Many marinas offer berths for sail and power boats. Even if you do not have or want to rent your own boat, there are many enjoyable cruises and tour boats along the harbor.

North Beach is a well-known and favorite spot. The annual Air and Water Show at this location attracts an estimated audience of two million people over a two-day period. The show is the oldest and largest free air and water exhibition in the United States.

The Oak Street Beach is possibly Chicago's most popular stretch, especially along the part where the shoreline curves. There is a concrete breakwater on the southern part of this beach which is a busy promenade on hot summer nights.

North Avenue Beach seems to be a favorite spot for families. Down at the southern end of the stretch however, is the hot spot for beach volleyball during both the summer and fall seasons. All of the many beaches along Chicago's lakefront are well loved and used. Locals and visitors alike recognize that this is a place for fun in the sun and water.

Swimming, sunning, boating — whatever you desire, Chicago offers all the elements for a great summer.

Sell-out crowds at the Skyline Stage, on Navy Pier, enjoy views of the lake, skyline and unforgettable performances of many kinds.

Navy Pier

While Navy Pier is a modern and exciting attraction, it is also an historic one. The Pier opened to the public back in 1916 as the largest construction of its kind in the world and the only pier to mix business with pleasure. Between then and now, Navy Pier, named so in 1927 as a tribute to Navy personnel who served during World War 1, has hosted numerous events and has been home to many organizations. With a history that included housing several groups during World War I to becoming a facility for the University of Illinois and from hosting the city's first Holiday Folk Festival to acting as a convention and trade show center, Navy Pier was designated a Chicago landmark in 1977.

Today, after a $150 million redevelopment project in 1994, Navy Pier features shopping promenades, restaurants, indoor and outdoor gardens, a convention center, IMAX theatre, live theatre, a family pavilion including the Chicago Children's Museum, an amusement park and more. Navy Pier offers over 50 acres of attractions of every kind and still serves as a port.

The Carousel, found by the Ferris wheel, adds yet another touch of class and fun to a day at Navy Pier.

Navy Pier is home to the world's first Ferris wheel. It made its debut in Chicago at the 1893 Colombian Exposition. This old friend has 40 gondolas to take riders up 15 stories — a great way to see the skyline of the city.

Navy Pier is a world-class landmark and attraction that features enough variety of food, entertainment and shopping to please everyone.

There's much to do at Navy Pier in the winter, including a visit to the magnificent Crystal Gardens — a massive 32,000 square-foot, indoor botanical park. The gardens are glass enclosed and offer a day in the topics.

The Chicago Children's Museum is designed specifically for young children, with many things to see, do and touch.

SHOPPING

Serious shoppers love Chicago because of its **"Magnificent Mile"** of truly fabulous shops, malls and boutiques — it's the city's most glamorous shopping thoroughfare.

The Magnificent Mile stretches from 400-1,000 North Michigan Avenue. There are over 180 shops and boutiques in the **Water Tower Place** and at 900 North Michigan Avenue Shops, both atrium shopping malls. The magnificence continues at **Chicago Place,** home to over 80 distinguished stores, and Michigan Avenue is also where to find the famous **Nike Town,** Gucci, Tiffany, and **Crate & Barrel** stores.

Shopping in Chicago is not only fun and plentiful, but historical too — State Street, in the Loop, allows for shopping in two of the city's oldest department stores — **Marshall Field & Co.** and Carson Pirie Scott.

(above) Part theater, part basketball court, part museum — Nike Town Chicago, the company's second store to celebrate sports, is much more than a store.

(top right) Crate & Barrel's stunning glass house for glass and housewares.

(bottom right) Chicago Place, with its 80-storey tower, has specialty shops and a top floor food court that overlooks the city.

(left) Bloomingdales is always a hot spot.

(below) One of Marshall Field's legendary clocks.

Water Tower Place, an Atrium shopping mall, has been called the first "multi-storey urban shopping center". There is plenty of shopping here with two major department stores, Marshall Field's and Lord and Taylor, plus more than 125 stores, shops and boutiques. Some of the well-known and loved stores include: Armani Exchange, August Woman, Banana Republic, Disney Store, Lane Bryant and Saks Fifth Avenue.

The Water Tower Place also offers eight restaurants and seven cinemas. Getting from one floor to another is a treat with escalators and glass-enclosed elevators that rise up through an atrium with an abundance of greenery. Seven of its 74 stories are devoted to retail stores, which opened their doors to shoppers in 1975. The rest of the structure houses offices, a hotel and condominium apartments.

The Sheraton Chicago Hotel and Towers is quite possibly the most talked-about hotel because of it's dynamic location. Its address on E. North Water St. allows for beautiful views of the Chicago sky-line, Lake Michigan and the Chicago River. The hotel is also steps away from many attractions and much shopping.

The Chicago Marriott is located in the heart of the city on the Magnificent Mile. It is a 46-storey hotel with deluxe accommodations. Another attraction to the Marriott is the fact that it is within walking distance from Chicago's finest shopping.

HOTELS

Always book ahead when planning to stay in Chicago! There's no such thing as a slow season in the "Convention Capital of the World". The city is home to the world's largest convention center, McCormick Place. There are many fine hotels in the O'Hare Airport area due to the great number of conventions and meetings held in Chicago. But to see the "real" Chicago, hotels 20 miles to the southeast are a much better bet.

Business travelers can have the best of both worlds by staying downtown. Here they will be near the La Salle Street financial district and many other business oriented organizations while at the same time will be close to many of Chicago's attractions. Those whose main interest is shopping and fine dining, which Chicago certainly has a lot of, may prefer the Near North hotels along Michigan Avenue's Magnificent Mile. Really, Chicago's sights and attractions are accessible from any hotel. And there is a hotel in Chicago for everyone's budget.

Chicago Hilton and Towers.

Hyatt Regency Chicago on East Wacker Drive.

The distinguished Palmer House, built during the Roaring Twenties.

(left) "Flamingo," by Calder.
(right) The untitled Picasso.

ART

Mayor Richard J. Daley initiated Chicago's ongoing support of public art when he dedicated the untitled **Picasso** in the Richard J. Daley Civic Center Plaza in 1967. The occasion marked the beginnings of a cultural renaissance, during which artists were invited to transform the city into an outdoor gallery.

Chicago art is not just limited to the galleries. Alexander Calder's "Universe" adds dynamism to the granite lobby of the landmark Sears Tower. Another of his works, **"Flamingo,"** stands in sharp contrast to architect Mies van der Rohe's three dark steel and glass federal buildings. A perfect example of Chicago art is the hand-chipped stone and glass fragments that make up "The Four Seasons". This piece of art, one of many by Russian-born artist Marc Chagall, blends scenes of Chicago with naturalistic imagery.

Of the many outdoor sculptures throughout Chicago, the Chicago Picasso, as it is generally referred to, attracts the most attention from tourists and residents alike. It was quite simple how Picasso came to make the monumental sculpture — he was, about four years before the unveiling, simply asked. Picasso refused a fee for his work preferring to give the design and model as a "gift to the people of Chicago". Now it is enjoyed by the people of Chicago and everyone who visits there.

Executed from Picasso's 42-inch steel model, the finished sculpture is 50 feet high and weighs 162 tons. Many people are still amazed that the work of such a great artist is a permanent part of Chicago.

(right) Manet.
(below left) Seurat.
(below right) Renoir.

The Art Institute of Chicago houses an internationally acclaimed Impressionist and Post-Impressionist collection, but had more humble beginnings as an art school in 1879. The Institute's guardian lions are a part of the pleasure of visiting the attraction.

The Museum of Science and Industry offers hands-on learning about ancient to modern technologies.

MUSEUMS

Chicago has many fine museums, devoted to the arts, sciences, natural history and culture. The most popular include the **Art Institute of Chicago,** the Field Museum of Natural History and the **Museum of Science and Industry.**

The Art Institute, its entrance flanked by the familiar guardian lions, houses an internationally renowned collection of Impressionist and Post-Impressionist painting. The Field Museum of Natural History features many state of the art exhibits exploring the earth and its people. Among its life-size reconstructions are the Pawnee earth-lodge and the entrance to an Egyptian tomb. Tracing the history of the Universe is exciting and fascinating at The Field Museum where there are plenty of exhibits and workshops to experience. The Museum of Science and Industry is designed specifically for visitor participation — it's the fun way to learn.

Many of Chicago's museums do not charge an admission and of the ones that do, many name one day as a "no admission" day.

The Transportation Court in the Museum of Science and Industry features a United Airlines 727, Buchanan's "No. 999" Locomotive, the "Spirit of America" automobile and the Texaco #13 "Mystery Ship" airplane.

The John G. Shedd Aquarium is the world's largest indoor aquarium with more than 8,000 aquatic animals.

A diver hand feeds some of the 100 or so aquatic animals at the 90,000 gallon Coral Reef. Exhibits have included a hawsksbill sea turtle, barracudas and nurse sharks.

A replica of the famous brachiosaurus stands tall and mighty outside the Field Muesum. Some of the treasures in the Stanley Hall of the Field Museum include: Sue, the worlds largest and most famous T-Rex, the fighting African Bull elephants and the coffin and mummies of children of Myron.

Built in 1930, the original **Adler Planetarium** is a well known Chicago landmark. The unique structure, in the form of a dodecagon, was built of rainbow granite and crowned with a lead-covered copper dome. The 12-foot-high sundial sculpture, an accurate time piece, was installed in the outdoor entry plaza in 1980.

The exterior of the Planetarium isn't the only thing that's unique about this attraction. Anyone who ventures inside is in for an incredibly realistic multi-media Sky Show that will transport them to nearby planets, distant stars and different galaxies. The Adler exhibits are three floors of heaven to those who enjoy astronomy, space exploration, telescopes and navigation.

The **Chicago Children's Museum** offers a fun way to learn with creative, interactive exhibits and workshops. Permanent exhibits include: The Stinky Truth About Garbage, Wheelchair Skill Course, The Art and Science of Bubbles, and the Grandparents Exhibit.

The Chicago Children's Museum features many "touch and feel" exhibits.

MILLENNIUM PARK

Inaugurated in July of 2004, this 24.5-acre park in the downtown area boasts some of Chicago's finest architecture, monumental sculpture, and landscape design. From the 1850s until the late 20th century, the current site of **Millennium Park** belonged to the Illinois Central Railroad.

Grant Park was developed around the railroad, due to city planner Daniel Burnham's Plan of Chicago in 1909, which considered the railroad property untouchable. At the completion of Grant Park, the railroad remained an eyesore in its corner. In 1997, Mayor Richard M. Daley directed his staff to develop plans for a new music venue to be built over the tracks. It was in 1998 that the Millennium Park idea was first envisioned, with the mission of creating new parkland in Grant Park to cover the railroad and unsightly parking lots found along the lakefront. With Mayor Daley and architect Frank Gehry's involvement, Millennium Park became the most ambitious public undertaking in Chicago's history.

There are many attractions to take in at Millennium Park. The 925-foot **BP Bridge** connects Millennium Park with Daley Bicentennial Plaza, and provides incomparable views of the Chicago skyline. Or enjoy three other areas for walking; through the **Lurie Garden**, a 2.5-acre garden that pays homage to the city's motto, "Urbs in Horto" (City in a Garden), or the **Chase Promenade**, a three-block-long walkway lined with nearly 200 trees where one might enjoy exhibitions, festivals, and other family events, or through the **Boeing Gallery**, a formal, outdoor space for public art exhibitions.

Cloud Gate is a 110-ton elliptical sculpture that reflects the city's famous skyline and clouds above it, made from seamless stainless steel. Inspired by liquid mercury, it is among the largest of its kind in the world measuring 66 feet long and 33 feet high. A 12-foot arch provides a "gate" to the concave beneath the sculpture.

The **Wrigley Square and Millennium Monument** is another landmark in the park. The tree-lined area of Wrigley Square is an inviting area to relax on the lawn or go for a stroll. It is anchored by the Millennium Monument (Peristyle), a nearly full-sized replica of the original peristyle that stood in the same location from 1917 to 1953. The semi-circle row of Doric-style columns that rise nearly 40 feet supports the designation of Michigan Avenue as the landmark district. Etched in stone at the base of the monument are the names of the founders of Millennium Park. Admission is free to come enjoy the park; tickets can be booked for events at the Harris Theatre. Walking tours are available.

The **Crown Fountain** is another sight to behold at Millennium Park. Consiting of two 50-foot glass block towers at each end of a shallow reflecting pool, the Crown fountain projects video display images of the faces of chicago residents, and releases a cascade of water.

McCormick Tribune Plaza & Ice Rink has a 16,000-square-foot ice-skating rink that operates from November

to March (weather permitting), with skate rentals available. for music fans, the **Jay Pritzker Pavilion**, which stands 120 feet high, is an outdoor music venue with 4000 fixed seats, and the **Great Lawn**, which can hold another 7000 people. The Pritzker Pavilion holds free concerts and events, and is host to the annual Chicago Music Festival. Also located at Millennium Park, the **Joan W. & Irving B. Harris Theater for Music & Dance** opened in November of 2003 has become the prime indoor performance space in Chicago. It can seat 1,525 people for each performance. One might also choose to visit the four **Exelon Pavillions**, which host the Park Welcome Center and gift shop.

Fittingly, for a city whose motto is "Urbis in Horto" or "City in a Garden," Chicago contains more than 6,500 acres of parkland. The parks are well loved and well used. Also, thanks to the Lakefront Protection Ordinance, most of Chicago's 20-mile lakefront is parkland or beach, free for the public to use.

Grant Park is the park that was, in the late summer of 1968, filled with young people protesting the Vietnam War. A riot broke out and Mayor Daley gave the police the order to "shoot to kill." Investigations into that night later showed that it was a police riot, not the misbehavior of the noisy but non-physical protesters, that caused the violence to erupt.

Today, Grant Park is a beautiful place to appreciate the mix of gardens or to enjoy a game of tennis or softball. It's also home to many outdoor concerts and events.

Zoos

Meet the animals — it couldn't be better at Chicago's zoos. **The Brookfield Zoo** is known for its naturalistic multi-species exhibits and its international role in animal breeding and conservation. It has 24 major animal exhibits, including Habitat Africa!, and The Fragile Kingdom. **The Lincoln Park Zoo** is involved in many Species Survival Plans, which ensure the long-term survival of endangered species by maintaining genetic diversity within a captive population. Lincoln is home to 37 endangered species.

The serene Jackson Park Japanese Garden (below) was commissioned by the Japanese government as a resting spot for visitors at the World's Columbian Exposition in 1893.

SPORTS

Chicago is a sports lover's paradise for both spectators and athletes. The Chicago Park District maintains hundreds of tennis courts, many public golf courses and a jogging/bicycle path that extends about 20 miles along the lakefront. Lake Michigan makes swimming and boating a breeze and ice skating, during the winter months, is popular at many outdoor rinks. The city is home to many professional sports teams and boasts state of the art recreational facilities. Nestled in the Des Plaines River Valley, the privately owned **Cog Hill Golf and Country Club** is Chicago's only PGA tour stop. The **Arlington International Racecourse** is home to the annual Arlington Million.

Home of the Chicago Bears football team since 1971, the original Soldier Field, based on a Grecian model, opened in 1924 and has always been a center for many sporting events. In 2002 Soldier Field underwent significant renovations, re-opening in September 2003. The remodeled stadium is 151-feet tall, and features 61,500 seats.

THE BEARS

The **Chicago Bears,** of the National Football League, were the first U.S. football team to: practice daily, have their own team band and team song and broadcast games over the radio. The Bears originally played at Wrigley Field but have been based at Soldier Field, built as a war memorial, since 1924. They won the 1985/86 Super Bowl against the New England Patriots.

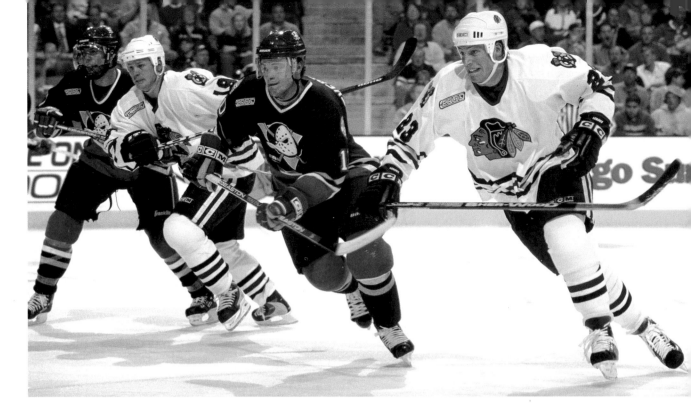

The Chicago Blackhawks have played at the United Center since 1994.

THE BLACKHAWKS

The **Chicago Blackhawks**, members of the National Hockey League since 1926, have won the Stanley Cup three times, the last in the 1960/61 season. The team moved from Chicago Stadium to the **United Center** in 1994. Several former Blackhawks are honored in hockey's Hall of Fame.

THE CHICAGO BULLS

The Chicago Bulls basketball team was founded in 1966. The Bulls have scored about 159,000 baskets over the past 30 plus seasons. They play their season from October to April at the United Center, 1901 West Madison Street. This popular team draws huge crowds; up to 23,000 fans pack the center to take in the action and entertainment of each game. Legendary Chicago Bulls star Michael Jordan, who wore number 23, made sporting history when he came out of early retirement on March 19, 1995. After playing a total of 13 seasons with the Bulls, Jordan officially retired again in 1999. He is considered one of the most gifted athletes in American sport. The Bulls logo and the celebrated number 23 can be seen on hats, shirts and jackets all over the world.

During the glory days of Michael Jordan, spectators watch the former Chicago Bulls guard display his talent.

Jordan, the six-foot-six-inch basketball marvel, is immortalized outside the United Center.

Wrigley Field.

THE CUBS AND WHITE SOX

Chicago is blessed with two professional baseball teams: the Chicago Cubs (National League) who play at **Wrigley Field** and the Chicago White Sox (American League) who call **New Comiskey Park** home. Built in 1914, Wrigley Field is one of the oldest ballparks in the major leagues and was the site of Babe Ruth's famous "called shot" home run, on Oct. 1, 1932. The White Sox were founded in 1900, won the 1906 and 1917 World Series and became the Western Division Champions in 1983 and 1993.

The baseball season begins around the first week in April and continues to early October.

New Comiskey Park.

Life in the neighborhood is filled with simple pleasures like pick-up ball on a summer's afternoon.

ENTERTAINMENT

Keeping yourself entertained in Chicago is merely a matter of choice — the options are unlimited. Although famous for its jazz and blues clubs, all types of music can be heard and enjoyed. A night at the theater can mean anything from a musical to a comedy, drama or dance. There are a wide variety of festivals, and free events are often sponsored by the city. Or simply take a walk to explore different neighborhoods.

The best way to get to know Chicago, as in any city, is to browse its streets. Of course you'll want to browse **The Loop**, but how about a stroll through the **Heart of Italy**, only minutes away from downtown. It is one of the oldest and most unique neighborhoods in the city. It is also an amazing treat if you enjoy traditional Italian cuisine served at its best.

Old Town, best known as the home of the Second City improvisational group, boasts one of the best and oldest summer art fairs in the United States. **Printer's Row** and **Burnham Park** are musts for anyone who didn't get enough architecture downtown. These neighborhoods feature restored buildings, jazz and blues clubs, shops, great bookstores and galleries.

Chicago gave the world "deep dish" pizzas and barbecued ribs, but with more than 6,000 restaurants, this city easily satisfies every possible gastronomic craving from haute cuisine to hot dogs. There are also a number of celebrity restaurants such as Michael Jordan's and Oprah Winfrey's. But to really sample the city's specialties visit the lakefront during the first week of July for **Taste of Chicago**, an annual festival featuring house specialties from dozens of eateries.

Grant Park is the center of many forms of summer entertainment. Aside from hosting the famous Taste of Chicago many enjoy annual treats like the well-known **Chicago Blues Festival** and, of course, the longest running festival at the park, the **Jazz Festival**.

(top) The always popular Hard Rock Cafe offers a high-energy tribute to rock music with classic American goodies to eat and plenty of star-studded memorabilia (above).

(left) Since 1998, the House of Blues is the place for live music and southern cuisine.

(top) The Annual Taste of Chicago takes place in July/August for two weeks. Samples, demonstrations and sales attract thousands of curious and hungry visitors.

(bottom) Harpo Studios is home to the Oprah Winfrey Show.

THEATRE

Over 100 theatre companies continually reaffirm the slogan, "See it first. See it best! See it in Chicago!" Dozens of professional and semi-professional theatres share resources and foster a permanent depth of talent recognized by Chicago's equivalent of the Tony Awards — the Joseph Jefferson Awards.

A "bastion of improvisation" for close to three decades, **The Second City** has become a comedic institution. Famed alumni include John Belushi, Shelly Long, Bill Murray, Joan Rivers and Alan Arkin.

The Chicago Theatre, the beautiful movie palace built in 1921, was saved from demolition by a civic-minded consortium and restored in 1986. It remains popular with the theatre-going crowd. Another place to enjoy a performance is the **Auditorium Theatre.** The superior acoustics in this 4,000 seat theatre are due in large part to the Chicago School design team of Dankmar Adler and Louis Sullivan, who built the multi-use facility in 1889.

(top left) The Second City has become a comedic institution.

(top right) Built in 1921, the Chicago Theatre was restored in 1986.

(above) The Auditorium Theatre, built in 1889, is a multi-use facility.

The League of Chicago Theatre maintains the HOT TIX booth in the city, which sells half-price, day-of-performance tickets for Chicago area theater, music and dance events.

Whether it is a familiar Beethoven symphony or a work being performed for the first time, concertgoers can expect the very best from the Chicago Symphony Orchestra when visiting Orchestra Hall, a National Historic Landmark building.

MUSIC

The **Chicago Symphony Orchestra** has invited classical music lovers to hear them perform, at Orchestra Hall, for more than a century. There are also several opera companies active within the city.

Chicago, best known for its jazz and blues legends, hosts annual festivals like the Chicago Blues Festival in Grant Park. The term "jazz" was created in Chicago in 1914, but the music itself had been moving up river from the South for some time. Many blues greats still call Chicago home and regularly play at local clubs like Buddy Guy's Legends and Blue Chicago. The Ravinia Festival is held annually in Highland Park, Illinois, 20 miles north of Chicago. It features many of the greatest names in jazz and the Chicago Symphony Orchestra.

The Civic Opera House is the home of the 40-year-old Civic Opera of Chicago as well as a few other large-scale performances. The Opera House seats about 3,400 people.

The Chicago Jazz Festival, which takes place in Grant Park, is an internationally recognized event which attracts afficionados from around the world to hear the best of traditional and contemporary jazz. The entire event, Chicago's longest running music festival, is the world's largest, free, outdoor jazz festival. Three days of jazz on three stages make for a great Labor Day weekend and mellow end to the summer. The Chicago Jazz Festival is an annual event.

Chicago is the place to be if you're into blues clubs. One of the many popular and well-known clubs is Blue Chicago. This club, located at 937 North State Street has a classic blues club atmosphere but is one of the roomier spots to hang out. Blue Chicago features a heavy lineup with local "meat-and-potatoes" bluesmen and women. The club features music nightly from 9 p.m. and is one of the few places that actually encourages dancing.

EDUCATION

The Chicago area has more than 50 colleges and universities, with a broad range of educational opportunities. The **Northwestern University**, founded in 1855, has a beautiful campus, the Evanston campus, that stretches along the lakefront for one mile. The schools of business, journalism, law and medicine are nationally known and respected. Its school of speech has graduated many leading actors as well.

The **University of Illinois** at Chicago is proud of a vast, modern, urban university campus. The buildings are grouped around an open amphitheater. Aside from being a great university, **Loyola** is Chicago's oldest university and largest Jesuit Institution in North America. The **University of Chicago** is now the Midwest's largest and most prestigious private academic institution.

Northwestern University.

University of Illinois.

The atomic age dawned on Chicago's south side in 1942, when Enrico Fermi's research team, at the University of Chicago, produced the first controlled nuclear chain reaction.

(top) Robie House, designed by Frank Lloyd Wright, is on campus.

(above) Another campus landmark is Henry Moore's bronze, "Nuclear Energy."

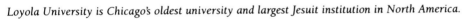

Loyola University is Chicago's oldest university and largest Jesuit institution in North America.

Chicago's O'Hare International Airport has held the title "World's Busiest Airport" for more than three decades.

O'Hare International Airport is 20 miles from downtown.

TRANSPORTATION

Chicago is the major Midwest hub for all modes of transport in central U.S., combining the last century's water and rail arteries with the 20th century's air and roadways. The Chicago Port Authority handles millions of tons of commercial goods annually, serving ships travelling the continent's major inland waterways.

Getting around Chicago itself is simple, the **Chicago Transit Authority** runs an extensive network of buses and the famous "El" or elevated/subway trains in the city and nearby suburbs. There are also commuter trains and buses between the city and suburbs. Don't rule out walking as an option — there's lots to see and do on a stroll in Chicago. Also, if you prefer, there are plenty of taxis, but remember they charge extra for each additional passenger!

Although the Elevated Trains in Chicago are well-known, transportation by trains goes way back in this city. The first railroad constructed out of Chicago, the Galena and Chicago Union, was chartered January 16, 1836, to connect Chicago with the lead mines at Galena. "The Pioneer," the first locomotive on the track, arrived after the charter was granted.

The railroad and the canal were vital in the development of Chicago as a city. The population tripled in the six years following the opening of the canal. Eventually other railroads were built and Chicago became and remains the largest railroad center in the world.

CONCLUSION

Explore Chicago's many facets and various moods — it's a city to be enjoyed. Pick up on the energy of busy city streets, relax in the park or at the beach. Expand your mind at the galleries and museums, stretch your credit in the many malls and shops, tantalize your taste buds in more than 6,000 restaurants, then feed your soul at the many music, theater and arts festivals.

You'll love Chicago — it's charming neighborhoods, bold architecture and fabulous entertainment. Its sights and sounds are like no other city. See for yourself.

Published and Distributed by

Irving Weisdorf & Co. Ltd.
2801 John Street,
Markham, Ontario, L3R 2Y8

Photo Editor	Writer	Designer
Hilary Forrest	**Kara Kuryllowicz**	**Jack Steiner**

Photography

Larry Fisher — 1, 2, 4, 8/9, 11, 12, 17b, 18a, 19, 20a, 22, 26/27, 28, 29b, 32b 34a, 35b, 38a, 39b, 40d, 51a, 52b, 53a, 53b, 54b, 58a, 58b, Front cover, Back cover

Alan Schein — 10

Irving Weisdorf & Co. Ltd. — 3, 5, 30, 31, 33c, 39a, 44/45, 49b, 60a, 60b, 62b, 62d 62d, 62e, 63a, 63b, 63d, 63f

The Image Bank
John Bryson — 36a
Guiliano Colliva — 61
David W. Hamilton — 17a, 55b
Gregory Heisler — 20b, 52a, 57b
David Maenza — 16a, 24, 25
Andrea Pistolesi — 13b
Marc Romanelli — 16b
Santi Visalli — 56b, 59c

Tony Stone Images
Glen Allison — 43b
Churchill & Klehr — 34b
David Hanson — 23
Cathy Melloan — 21
Peter Pearson — 37c
Mark Segal — 15
Charles Thatcher — 57a

Gera Dillon — 13a, 14

Gerald D. Tang — 53d

Ray Grabowski — 48a, 48b, 49a, 50b

Stephen Green — 51b

Ivy Images — 6, 7

Kim Karpeles — 40a, 40b, 42a

Larry Okrent — 42b

Mike Smith — 48d

Ken Tanaka — 43e

Johnny Iaquinta — 43a

MLB Photos — 51c, 51d

NBA Photos
Noren Trotman — 50a

Superstock/Four by Five Photography Inc. — 37a, 37b, 37d

Photos below provided courtesy of the following organizations:

Adler Planetarium	41a, 41b
Arlington International Race Course	47b, 47c
Auditorium Theatre	55c
Bloomingdale's	33a
Blue Chicago Club	57c
Chicago Board of Trade	63c
Chicago Children's Museum	41c
Chicago Department of Aviation	60c
Chicago Department of Cultural Affairs	36b, 37c, 62a
Chicago Park District	43c, 43d, 46d, 62g, 63e
Crate & Barrel	32a
Chicago Zoological Society/ Brookfield Zoo	46a, 46c
Edward G. Lines Jr./ Shedd Aquarium	39c
Hyatt Regency Chicago	35b
James Steere/Chicago Symphony Orchestra	56a, 62c
Mike Klemme/GOLFOTO	47a
Loyola University, Chicago	59d
Marshall Field's	33b
Mayor's Office of Special Events	54a
Museum of Science and Industry	38b
Nike Town	32c
Palmer House	35c
The Field Museum, Chicago	40c, 40d
The Second City	55a, 62f
University of Chicago	59a, 59b
University of Illinois	58c

(Also available in French, German, Spanish, Italian and Japanese)

Copyright © 1995 **Irving Weisdorf & Co. Ltd.**

Printed in Korea